LEARNING TO LIVE

Learning to Live

A selection of writings
By M. H. Tester

Compiled by Stephen Castro

Psychic Press Ltd
20 Earlham Street, London WC2H 9LW

ISBN 0 85384 059 8

Printed in Great Britain

CONTENTS

INTRODUCTION

THERE was once a man who bought a book on body-building. When he finished reading it he wrote to the author saying: "I have read your book. Will you now please send me the muscles?"

Even in these alleged enlightened times there remains a primitive assumption the mere reading of a book, especially when concerned with matters such as self-development and healthy living, will magically endow the reader with the objectives contained within it.

"Learning to Live" is a book designed to provide the reader with a series of experimental directions which can act as a corrective to those disabling attitudes that are the causes behind much of today's physical ailments and mental and emotional despair.

Thus shall the reader be better equipped to perceive and respond to those extra dimensions of life which we may loosely term as spiritual. I say loosely because until the "spiritual" becomes a reality based on personal experience and not just a word to excite or to provide emotional stimuli we can only use it in the sense of an hypothesis.

To achieve such ends requires a commitment from *you*.

Reading this book and then pronouncing abracadabra will not bring you health, fulfilment, wisdom, spirituality or any other of the possibilities that await the man or woman who has successfully learnt how to live.

But careful reflection upon what has been written, with an endeavour to attempt to put into practice the helpful hints and commonsense advice provided by M. H. Tester, could well transform your whole life.

S. Castro

Chapter One

FULL CIRCLE

I SUPPOSE, due to my outlook on life, I could be called a mystic. Maybe I do not look like one, but few mystics did or do. I was not always a mystic. When I was a teenager I found myself completely unsatisfied by my orthodox religion. It gave me no spiritual satisfaction. It presented a dogma and credo I could not accept. The assumptions were unproven. The theology left me confused.

I became convinced either I was on the wrong track or if I was on the right one it had become distorted and overlaid to the point of making it unrecognisable and even dangerous. I decided to look elsewhere.

For many years, including the troubled times of World War II, I sought the truth. I held discussions with priests of most Christian sects. I listened to rabbis, Jesuits, agnostics and humanists. I visited churches, mosques, synagogues and temples.

Always a prolific reader I ploughed through the theology of the western world, the east and even the far north. I studied strange creeds and outlandish beliefs. Some I could not understand. Others I did, but could not accept.

By the time I was 30 I had rejected them all. I used a rough and ready philosophy that generally worked out in practice. When in doubt I examined my conscience. If that failed I just muddled through.

They say life begins at 40. It did for me. But first I was struck down by a spinal condition. A disc in my lower back became grossly displaced. I was in great pain.

My spine was distorted. My hip was inches out of true. One leg was nearly an inch shorter than the other and I had to wear a built-up shoe. My right leg was in agony; my foot had almost lost all feeling.

My torso was encased in a spinal jacket, originally of canvas, leather and steel. When this failed to help, one of quarter inch thick rigid plastic was moulded to my body.

I could find no position in which I could be free of pain. It was impossible to stand, sit or lie down without pain. To walk, even with a stick, was agonising. I could not drive a car.

My day was full of coloured capsules. Every hour I had to take some form of drug. These were two kinds of tranquillisers, painkillers and sleeping pills. The table by my bed was like a pharmacy.

I tried to take a holiday, but the French beds made it so bad I had to be flown home as an emergency patient after a few days. An ambulance met the plane. In hospital followed weeks of traction, more drugs, the suggestion of a bigger, better orthopedic jacket. After a couple of years I was just where I had started.

Then I rebelled. I insisted on seeing the top man in the country. I wanted to know. Was I to spend the rest of my life a cripple? Was there any hope?

The top man was a physician in Wimpole Street who had written the medical text book on my complaint. He was charming, thorough and very positive.

He confirmed the previous diagnosis and told me the spinal distortion was now massive. He recommended an immediate operation as otherwise he could not answer for my retaining the use of my right foot.

The operation was to be performed at a critical point in my back near the junction of the spinal nervous system. It would have to be done by a neurosurgeon. The probability of success was under 40 per cent. Could I enter the clinic that afternoon for an immediate operation?

No I could not! With a wife and five children, a professional office and other responsibilities, I needed time to make a decision. If I decided to have the operation I required time to arrange it.

It was October. The specialist said he would give me until Christmas. After that he would not answer for my foot. He would write to my doctors and confirm the diagnosis and his recommendations.

A taxi took me to my office. The kindly driver helped me inside. It was lunch time. My secretary was out. The telephone engineer was pottering in my office. I sat at her desk, put my head in my hands and brooded.

I was at the end of my tether. Two years of agony, discomfort, inconvenience and frustration. Now I was faced with a major operation with a low success factor. The telephone rang. I ignored it. It kept on ringing. Nobody answered it. Eventually I picked up the receiver more to shut it up than anything.

The man on the telephone was a business acquaintance. I had not spoken to him for some time. He was ringing about a minor commercial matter. I was, as I have said, at the end of my tether.

I suppose it showed in my tone, for he asked me what was wrong. There comes a time when you have to share your burden. His was a sympathetic voice. So I told him.

His response was surprising. No sympathy, no platitudes, but instead a positive suggestion. Would I see a man who could help me if he arranged it? Would I? This was more than a straw to clutch at; it was a helping hand.

I did not then know the man I saw that evening was a spiritual healer. I did not know what a spiritual healer was. In fact I do not believe I had even heard of such people.

The story of how I was healed has already been written.* By Christmas I was free of pain. My body was upright, my spine undistorted, my hip in its original position and both legs the same length.

I went back to the specialist. As he examined me he became more and more amazed. Eventually he was satisfied I was healed. There was some slight residual weakness. I might experience a sciatic twinge or two, but these would clear up. I was healed—no stick, no spinal jacket, no operation. I was healed. So I told him!

When I went back to the healer to thank him he informed me that I, too, had the gift of healing. I should develop it.

* "The Healing Touch," Psychic Press.

From that moment doors I never knew existed began to fly open. I learned about Spiritualism. The more I learned the more I found I already knew. Life was a succession of places that should have been strange to me but which were familiar. After seeking, I had found.

A great reservoir of spiritual awareness and psychic knowledge flowed through me as the healing opened the floodgates. I knew why I was here and what I had to do. The fallacies and superstitions of orthodox religions became the games of the nursery as the wide open road of spiritual maturity appeared before me.

Now I am a spiritual healer. I heal bodies and reorientate souls. The sick and the weary come to me with their tales of woe. I treat them, spin them round, point them in the right direction and open the door of spiritual awareness.

One day the telephone rang. It was the same business acquaintance who had sent me to the healer. Would I see a man he knew who needed help? An appointment was arranged.

He was in pain with a slipped disc in the lower back. His hip was out of true, his spine distorted. He had sciatica in his leg and foot.

Here was a man with all the symptoms I had endured for two years. I said little as I put my hand on his back and felt the healing force flowing. But inwardly I felt an enormous glow of fulfilment.

The wheel had turned a full circle. The pattern of my own illness, my healing and the spiritual revelation that followed was clear.

Nearly everybody who visits a healer is suffering

from a medically incurable disease. There is invariably a long list of treatments, drugs and suffering. The tale generally ends with the statement, "The doctor told me I would have to learn to live with it."

The patient has found he cannot live with it. He is at the end of his tether, often in pain, incapacitated and unhappy. Through a friend, or a friend's friend, or somebody who knows a person who was healed, he gets a healer's name and writes for an appointment.

Most patients who come to see me have no idea what a healer is. They are confused, unhappy and clutching at straws. Many of them think I am a faith healer and hasten to tell me they believe in me. Perhaps for the benefit of those who need healing, and for those who can help in this connection, I should tell what happens when you visit a healer.

Let us get our terms of reference straight. What is a faith healer? He is a man who can generate in a patient such faith that the self-restoring mechanism which everybody has is revived—and the patient heals himself. So much of today's sickness is psychosomatic that often this is enough.

If a sick person can be convinced a faith healer can heal him, and he believes deeply he will get well, then he probably will. But I am not a faith healer. I am a spiritual healer.

A spiritual healer is a healing medium. When a patient comes to me, I heal him when I am in a light trance. I use the words "light trance" because I think this explains what happens. But it is difficult to put into words any form of psychic experience.

The healing that flows through me is directed by my

healing guides. I like a patient to tell me in detail what his problem is. The guides can then hear at first-hand and assess the treatment that is needed.

As the story unfolds a pattern emerges. I learn of frustration, disappointment, self-pity and eventual desperation. Many of the diseases are emotionally induced. But the treatment does not vary if the disease is psychosomatic or functional.

I let the patient talk his fill. I then explain I am not a doctor, that I have no medical qualifications, that I am a spiritual healer. I tell him I can guarantee no cure, that I do not know if I can heal him, how long it will take, how many visits may be necessary.

What I do tell him is that I regard each healing session as an experiment. I make no charge. If he is happy to accept what is to take place as an experiment between friends, that is as far as I will go. I promise him nothing. But I give him hope.

I ask the patient to remove only his outer garments. I sit him on a chair or a stool. In an atmosphere of calm and quiet, I place my right hand on his forehead, my left on the nape of his neck. In this position I then seek attunement.

Attunement is the first stage of my trance. It is almost a state of day-dreaming. I feel I am drifting away, leaving my body and mind open to my guides to use as a healing vehicle. I regard myself as a receiving set. Through me passes the healing force. All I have to do is to leave the channel pure and open.

When I first started healing, it used to take me ten or 15 minutes to reach a state of attunement. But after some years' practice, I can "tune myself in" very quickly. Now the process takes only a few seconds.

I am standing in a day-dream, my hands resting lightly on the patient, my mind elsewhere, my thoughts virtually non-existent. In this state my healing guides are able to work through me direct to the patient, and to heal.

If the patient is suffering from pain, or some deformity, or a disease which has its symptoms in a specific part of the body, I may well also lay my hands there. But this is more to comfort than to heal.

People react in different ways. Most become sleepy and relaxed. Those who suffer from arthritic conditions often tell me that where my hand has rested there is great warmth. Whatever the patients' reactions, they leave me happier than when they came.

In my state of attunement, I am not aware of much that is going on. I can be brought out of it if, for instance, my telephone rang. That is why the bell is switched off and nobody is allowed to interrupt me. Normal noises do not penetrate. I ask the patient to be quiet and not to speak.

The actual time of a healing session is seldom more than ten minutes. It often stretches to half an hour because the patient tells me a long story. And when the healing is over he wants to know a little more of what is happening to him.

I have dispensed completely with any form of ritual, rite or religious symbolism.

If I get a nervous patient, I find sometimes it relaxes him to play a little music. Where I have not the time or the facilities it does not seem to make any difference.

Too many patients are run down and in a poor state

of health. Initially, it is necessary to improve their general condition. After one or maybe two visits, the patient is much brighter, sleeping better, eating well, has a clearer eye, and accepts a more philosophical view.

Often the symptoms of the disease are still present and there is no specific change. But there is a recognisable improvement in his attitude. Then the healing becomes specific. The symptoms and the disease itself clear up often remarkably quickly.

I do not know how long it will take for a patient to be healed—or if he will be healed at all. I am neither clairvoyant nor clairaudient. Sometimes I do possess "the ability of knowing." But I am not always certain I interpret what I "know" as opposed to what I wish.

Even if the healing is spontaneous I ask the patient to come back the following week so I may judge the progress.

It is not within my power to choose who shall get better. I am glad this is so. My responsibility would be too great were it otherwise. As it is, my sole responsibility is to be available for all who ask for healing.

I keep myself physically and mentally as immaculate as possible. What happens subsequently is a matter for the patient and for the healing guides who do the work. I know my guides because they have spoken to me.

From time to time, I sit with a medium in case there is a message I should be receiving. It enables me to learn whether what I am doing is considered correct or if there should be some variation in the practice I adopt.

I do not have any sacred symbols. I have no orthodox

religious affiliations. It does not matter to me whether the man I heal is a devout Roman Catholic, a Moslem, a Hindu or a Jew, or whether he is a Chinese Communist completely without acceptance of God, or an African with a tribal religion.

Healing is not an end in itself; it is a means. When people come to me for help, they are in need not only of physical healing but also of spiritual reorientation. You can preach to a man until you are hoarse and convince him of nothing.

Once he has been healed of a painful, inconvenient and medically incurable disease, his mind is open to the power that is waiting. That man will want to know more. He will wish to investigate the power that made him well. So I open the door to spiritual awareness.

I regard this opening of doors as being the more important part of my work. Francis, who is my favourite saint, had a little prayer which I say often. It goes like this:

Lord please grant that where there is error I may bring truth,
That where there is doubt I may bring faith,
That where there is despair I may bring hope,
That where there are shadows I may bring Thy light,
That where there is sadness I may bring joy.

I accept no reward. I believe that what I am doing is the function I was sent here to perform. This in itself is enough. I am fortunate in having sufficient worldly goods at the moment to be free from the need to charge patients.

It is a reward in itself that I am able to perform the

18

function of a healer. St Francis had another prayer which I think does sum it up:

Lord grant that I may seek to comfort rather than to
    be comforted,
To understand than to be understood,
To love than to be loved,
For it is by giving that one receives,
It is by self-forgetting that one finds,
It is by forgiving that one is forgiven,
It is by dying that one awakes to eternal life.

Chapter Two

LIFE'S GRAND DESIGN

I GET a lot of letters. Most are written by people wanting healing. But many are from bewildered men and women seeking truth. I help them to the extent I can. Sometimes it would be comforting if I had somebody to write to. If I did I would ask different questions from those I get asked.

The earth is a minute part of the cosmos. In outer space there are other suns, galaxies and planets. Who or what created them all?

If you can imagine the whole universe, or just look at a snowflake under a microscope, you see a design. If there is a design there must have been a designer. If we call him "God" it is reasonable to assume he made us. As well as the rest. He wanted intelligent life to come into being. Why? Why have we been created? What is God's purpose?

An atheist denies God's existence. Yet he will accept the "big bang" theory of how the world started. Most scientists today also accept it. Yet "big bang" is just another term for creation. Who made the bang? Who unleashed the enormous force that produced the original cosmic explosion? And what was there to explode in the first place? And who created that?

These are some of the questions I would ask if I had somebody to write to.

When you watch a flock of starlings wheeling through the sky, they change course suddenly and then twist and turn in a complex display of aeronautics. They do this as one living unit, not as individual birds. It is as though they become part of one organism with a central intelligence.

You see a similar happening with a shoal of fish. Insects seem to have this intelligent unification. Bees and ants behave as one organism, each doing its part. Even in an emergency they perform acts not previously done in unity.

Maybe all life started that way. Perhaps once upon a time life was a central organism. The big bang scattered it into billions of parts. We are moving away at a fantastic speed from the original explosion centre. We can no more get an answer to where we are going than a piece of shrapnel can after a grenade has exploded.

In Japan, about the middle of the 18th century, an artist called Hokusai painted a giant mural using a barrel of ink and a broom. Then to demonstrate his versatility he painted two sparrows on a single grain of rice.

There are billions of life forms to which those two sparrows on a grain of rice seem like a mural. And there are billions more of life forms so minute that the ones small enough to liken the painting on the grain of rice as a mural seem like giants by comparison.

The enormous empty wastes of the Atlantic or the sands of the Sahara give us impressions of the vastness of the planet earth. But earth is a small planet in a solar system that is part of a galaxy. And our galaxy is part of a planetary system and a small part at that. There are thousands upon thousands of planetary systems and millions of planets. The strongest telescopes we have can see only a minute portion of this corner of space.

One of the very small things we can imagine is, perhaps, the atom. But the atom itself is a solar system. When we have microscopes strong enough perhaps we shall find life forms in this system.

The mind boggles. It cannot imagine space that is infinite in size and has no basis for comparison, or minuteness that is below microscopic vision.

Yet many scientists regularly study these things. There are people to whom the electron microscope is a tool in daily use. Others man radio telescopes focused on some point in space from which they are picking up signals.

Whether we study the vastness of space or the smallness of life there is one common factor. We find everywhere a design. The intricacies of nuclear organisation or the complexities of galactic interaction all seem to be part of a grand design. We are only now starting to comprehend the ingenuity of our small portion of it. This is understandable since man is still at a primitive stage in his evolutionary scale.

Each and every one of us is born at a different level of spiritual awareness; there are as many levels as there are people. Each is advancing at his own rate. Therefore, each of us must seek to find our road and travel on it as far as we are equipped to do so. The healer's function is to indicate where the road can be found, and at times to act as a signpost.

I am prepared to tell people what I believe. But I am not an evangelist. I seek to convert nobody. What you believe is uniquely your responsibility. Look for spiritual truths. Seek personal knowledge. What you discover for yourself you will remember. What you are told is secondhand and has not the same value.

My personal credo is a simple one.

There is a theory advanced by psychiatrists that God is but a fantasy of the human mind. I disagree fundamentally with this. I disagree too with those who visualise the deity as a father figure, as an elderly gentleman with a white beard and a kind of nightdress who has a bad memory and has to be constantly reminded of our needs. To me God exists.

Whether you call this God, the Great Spirit or the life force is purely a matter of semantics.

Scientists are finding greater sources of creative energy in this world. There is no limit seemingly to the energy we can release from the atom, the sun, the tides and from other and as yet hardly appreciated sources. Topping it all is the energy of life itself.

God exists. To me he, she or it is pure energy allied to creative design.

Each of us is linked with this divine energy. Each of us is a spirit occupying a body for a short while, but with an indivisible link with God. Each spirit is everlasting. In different lives its format may change. But the hard core that is the soul is linked with the source of life and energy just as every drop of water is part of the ocean.

Your life here has a purpose. I will go further; all life has a purpose. You may not see the pattern that applies

23

to you. Many never do. But to discern this pattern is your primary function in this life and to go along with it.

Most unhappiness, most frustration and most ill-health are due to a person failing to see this design or in seeking to impose on it a pattern foreign to it.

Life is not bestowed as a random gift. It has purpose. You may not be able to find the complete plan. In fact, I doubt if you ever will. But be assured the plan exists. Find out as much about it as you can. Go along with it. Your spiritual evolution is the name of the game.

Your life here by most standards is short. Do not use this as a criterion, for all life is continuous. People are born and die. You may see the beginnings of life and what you think is the end, not only in people but in animals, plants and even ideas.

What you see is an illusion. Life is a process that goes on forever. The format may change, but life continues. There is no halting. We either progress at the right rate, or by our own actions slow it down so it may seem that we regress. But the evolutionary progress of life is a fact. It is endless and progressive. You are a part of this divine scheme.

Because life is a continuous process it needs to operate according to natural laws. This is inevitable. The laws are intricate. They are unfailing. Natural laws cannot be broken, cannot be amended, cannot be repealed. They are immutable.

There are many laws. They are not written down in holy books, or carved out of stone tablets. You have to ascertain them yourself. Some of the orthodox religions have discovered a few of these laws and sought to enshrine them. Remember, what you find out for yourself you know. What you are told may be suspect at some time.

Discover for yourself how the laws of cause and effect operate. Maybe you have. Ponder on your own experiences that have demonstrated the law that "like begets like." Think upon what has happened to you and ask if you have "sown indeed what you have reaped." Look back and learn. Then look up and profit by it.

The natural laws are unfailing in their operation. You will violate many of them. You may not be aware of some until you have transgressed them and seen the results. If in doubt remember the basic rule that love fulfils the law. It is love for your fellows, for all creatures, for life itself that brings understanding of the laws closer to you.

You have been given one incomparable gift. It is a measure of free will. Your will is a great force. It gives you the power to go against nature, to take the wrong road, to project your efforts in a direction that is not right for you.

It also has no equal in the world when it is directed towards correct living, spiritual advancement and love. As in all things it is up to you. Do not blame others. You made your choice. You are responsible. You can never be a victim. You are the master of your soul and of your destiny.

These are the things I believe. I am human, weak and fallible. I do not live fully up to my ideals. But I hope that I am improving all the time.

I am not a guru. I am not a teacher. I am a simple man on whom has been bestowed the gift of healing.

The responsibility of how you live, how you think and the attitudes you adopt are uniquely yours and yours alone.

I am suspicious of those who claim to know all the answers. It is in the nature of man to over-simplify. To explain an abstract he needs concrete words. This he can manage to do only by bringing everything down to his own level.

Thus, we have the simple explanations of orthodox religions. They seek to make the infinite finite, to present God as a person, to set out a code of rules for conduct and belief that cover all eventualities. They claim theirs is the only way to spiritual evolution.

The rules have been worked out over a long period. They say they are all divinely inspired. Many are based on the effect of a clear conscience for the man who obeys them. He feels better. He has no doubts because he has conformed. Those who say they understand these things have told him so.

The man who does not conform does not feel happy or well. His conscience troubles him. He may get ill or even die prematurely. Such is the power of suggestion and the result of brainwashing.

And this does not only apply to the African witch-doctor. It can be seen today as the lapsed Roman Catholic struggles with his conscience; in the Jew who has largely forsaken his faith, but cannot resist going to the synagogue on the holy days, or performing some of the rituals his father practised.

Such is the extent of the influence of the orthodox that people are happier if they have blind faith and slavishly follow rites they are told are essential to their salvation. That their spiritual development is being stunted is glossed over in the general euphoria of conformance.

A group of children all doing the same exercise in school and singing the same simple song are the greatest conformists. No child likes to be the odd one out. When they grow up the same childish need is exploited.

A church congregation generates the same smug euphoria, the same comfort of belonging to a group activity. To this is added the righteous feeling of being in the right, as their priests have assured them. Any deviation can be forgiven. The confessional has the same function as the psychiatric couch.

This might have done for an illiterate peasant community in the Middle Ages. But with universal education has come more than the ability to read. People have learned to reason.

The orthodox religions are seen for what they are, a facile and fabricated system for imprisoning people's souls, and controlling their thinking, wealth, loyalties and often their very lives.

Try clearing your mind of what you have been taught about religion. It will not be easy. But pick up any book of prayer, whatever your religion, and read it for the first time in an analytical way.

You will find that nearly all prayers are based on an interpretation of God as a man. He is generally a patriarchal figure. He is visualised as an old, wise man.

To him you pray for the things you selfishly need. As a preamble to most orthodox prayers is the personal reference you have to offer. You remind him you are a good person; you are a fully-paid up member of his church; you have been true to the rules.

Then you ask for the things you want. Sometimes you have to remind him of the things he has overlooked. You ask for rain. Perhaps he missed your need in this area. You ask for health. Maybe he does not know you have arthritis.

You ask for wealth, for a child, for the love of somebody, for the return of a relative, for the safety of people in peril. And in wartime you ask for the death and destruction of your enemies. You may even join in asking for the blessing of a ship and all who sail in her, when it is a submarine or a destroyer designed to deal out death and destruction on an enormous scale.

A little intelligent thought will show you how stupid these prayers really are. If there is a God then he is omnipotent, all-seeing and all-knowing, that means he knows what is going on everywhere.

He does not need to be reminded like an elderly father with an ailing memory. He does not need to have his oversights pointed out to him, like a computer with a malfunction in the memory bank. He does not need to have you identify yourself and to tell him you are on his side. The assumption is blasphemy.

Yes, I do believe in God. I do not see him as a person, yet I see him in everything, in every living person, animal and plant. I go further. I do not only believe there is a God. I *know* there is.

Do I pray? Yes I do. I have two prayers that I say often. The first is, "Thy will be done." My life is a constant process of trying to attune myself to his will, to put myself in harmony with the life force, to feel and know the bliss of being at one with nature and the power that fills it.

Many times I fail. But sometimes, when I am healing or when I am in meditation, I find this deep attunement.

It is part of everyone's spiritual development. We need no churches, synagogues, rituals, mystic rites, special clothes, instruments or times.

God is not only in those "holy places" or with those who claim a sole right to him. He is within you. He is in your house. He is in and with every living thing. Be still and know that it is so.

My second prayer is even shorter. It is simply, "Thank you." I cannot understand why an earthquake or any other catastrophe should be called "an act of God."

To me a sunset is an act of God. A baby is an act of God. A daisy or a snowdrop is an act of God. I am an act of God. And for the wonderful lives we lead, the love and happiness we share, the sunshine and the food and drink we enjoy, for the knowledge and understanding, for art, music, ecstasy and tears, I say "Thank you."

I am suspicious of those who claim to know all the answers. Me, I do not even know all the questions!

Chapter Three

WESTERN ORTHODOX
RELIGION EXAMINED

I AM convinced one reason why the world is in its present stage must be due to the way the Church held back all spiritual, philosophical and scientific growth for a thousand years.

During the Dark Ages the Church imposed a Mafia-like control on the minds, imagination, spiritual and psychic life and on the material growth of all people.

Those with psychic ability were burnt at the stake or tortured. Thus psychic ability, largely hereditary, was virtually stamped out. Philosophy, other than the Church's rigid official doctrines, was banned.

Science, treated as witchcraft, was ruthlessly exterminated where possible. The Church held western civilisation in an iron grip – and held it back, too.

The objective was for none to have the education, knowledge, authority or ability to challenge its all-powerful stranglehold.

We have lost a thousand years of progress, scientific research, psychic development and spiritual evolution.

Orthodox religion has caused more misery, wars,

deaths, suffering, insecurity and ignorance than any other single cause.

It is time this was recognised.

I read the Bible quite often. I like it. The stories are exciting. The characters become alive. The philosophy in parts is wonderful. The picture of life is true in many respects today.

I have a clear picture of Jesus in my mind. I see him as a gifted psychic and a man spiritually well in advance of his times. I visualise him as a rebel against the pomp, rituals and bigotry that surrounded him.

He wanted no riches here on earth. He strove for spiritual truth and the abandonment of the lip service and hypocrisy that had replaced true worship.

Let us examine a few of the true facts concerning the life of Jesus.

The Christian religion began with the man whom we call Jesus. He lived in Nazareth. He was an orthodox Jew. He rebelled against the religious strictness of his time. He was an agitator. As the country he lived in was a Roman province, called Judea, it had a governor. His name was Pontius Pilate. He was governor from AD 26–36. Jesus made such a nuisance of himself the governor had him executed.

People spoke about him after he had died. They wove stories about him. Eventually those stories were edited, altered, added to and were written down. They are now called the Gospels.

There is nothing new in the Gospels. Jesus was probably a member of a Jewish sect called Essenes. His teachings are very much like theirs. The Essenes were healers. They believed in life after death, selling all their goods to give to the poor, and that wealth and owning things hindered their spiritual growth. They lived a monastic life of holiness, gentleness and purity, sacrificing worldly pleasures for spiritual happiness.

The Gospels were written a long time after Jesus died; there were no tape recorders, or books (except holy scrolls) and not many means of recording what was said in Jesus' day. So the writers of the Gospels (who-ever they might have been) had to get most of their ideas as to how a god should act from other religions.

The Sermon on the Mount, for instance, consists of a lot of quotations from the Jewish psalms and proverbs strung together. The Lord's Prayer was taken from an old Jewish prayer. The Jews, in their turn, took it from an older religion of the Chaldeans.

The whole of the Gospels have been copied, bit by bit, from other religions. For instance, the virgin birth, and all the miraculous things that were supposed to happen to Jesus, are much the same as those that occur-red to Buddha a long time before.

Perhaps the easiest way to explain it would be to play the "true-or-false" game. Let's try, shall we?

Jesus really existed. Probably true. There is no men-tion in history there was such a man, but there is other evidence. I think we can put a "true" for this one.

He was the son of God. False. He was the son of man, and said so. You and I are the sons of God. To that extent Jesus was, too. He was human and mortal.

He was born of a virgin. False. All the pagan gods were supposed to have virgin births. It was a legend that was tacked on to men whom people wanted to make into gods.

The rest of his story is true. False. There were many so-called "saviour gods" before Jesus with almost identical stories. Here is one:

"He was taken prisoner, was tried in the Hall of Justice, was scourged and then led away to the mount. With him were two thieves, one of whom was released. After his execution·the city broke out in tumult. His clothes were carried away and he went down into the mount and disappeared from life. A weeping woman saw him at the gate of burial. He was brought back to life."

This sounds very much like the story of Jesus. Yes it does, doesn't it? But it is the tale of Bel, a Babylonian god who existed nearly 2,000 years earlier.

Jesus was a healer. True. He was probably a member of the Essenes sect, and they were healers. There are many spiritual healers today.

He saw visions and heard voices. True. He was a medium. He was clairvoyant (saw visions) and clairaudient (heard voices). Many mediums have one or both of these abilities.

He was crucified on a cross. Probably false. Most of the fables about saviour gods tell of them being crucified. But one Gospel even says he was hanged from a tree. He was executed by the Roman governor. How it was done does not really matter.

The cross became the Christian symbol. False. There were no Christians at the time of Jesus since he was a Jew. When his followers needed a symbol they chose a fish. The cross was an old pagan symbol. It was adopted by Christians many years later. They took most of their religion from the old pagan ones.

Jesus rose from the dead. True. When you die all that happens is you leave your earthly body. Your spirit still lives on. You continue your life in the other world. Some people come back to help those still here, to give proof of life after death, and to spread truth where ignorance existed before. That is what Jesus did.

The Bible is true. False. Most of it was copied from the Babylonians, or from a number of pagan religions. Even the stories about Adam and Eve, the Flood, the Tower of Babel were current in Babylon, as was the story of Moses and the bullrushes, long, long before our Bible was written.

But there are great truths in the Bible. True. But not one of them is new. Look at these: "Return good for evil and overcome anger with love." That was written by Buddha. He also wrote, "He that would cherish me let him go and cherish his sick comrade."

"Do unto others as you would they should do unto you." This was said by Confucius.

"Whenever thou art in doubt as to whether an action is good or bad, abstain from it." This was said by Zoroaster a thousand years before Jesus.

"One who is injured ought not to return the injury, for on no account can it be right to do an injustice, and it is not right to return an injury, or to do any evil to any man, however much we may have suffered from him." This was said by Socrates 450 years before Jesus.

"Let us not listen to those who think we should be angry with our enemies, and who believe this to be great and manly. Nothing so praiseworthy, nothing so clearly shows a great and noble soul, as clemency and readiness to forgive." This was said by Cicero 70 years

34

before Jesus.

"If a man strike thee, and in striking thee drop his staff, pick it up and hand it to him again," was said by Krishna centuries before Jesus was born.

Every teaching of Jesus can be found in older writings. Most of them are in the "Bhagavad Gita," the sacred book of India, and in the writings of Seneca, Ovid, Aristotle, Epictetus, Plato and others.

Christianity was responsible for raising the moral level of the world. False. This is an illusion. By the sixth century we find all the schools of philosophy closed, all education and learning banned, the worst of paganism flourishing, the best destroyed, and Europe in a night of intense darkness that lasted for more than 1,000 years. The dark ages existed until people became intelligent enough to doubt the Church's teachings.

Christianity teaches tolerance and understanding. False. Historians have tried to add up the number of people murdered, executed, slaughtered, burned or tortured to death because they doubted the Christian Church's teachings. The nearest they can get is 25,000,000. Perhaps I had better write it down. The number is twenty-five million.

Jesus founded the Christian Church. False. It was founded by the Council of Nicaea. In AD 325, 2,048 ignorant, superstitious and power-hungry clergy met under the command of Constantine to decide what the Christian religion should and should not contain. Out of this assembly emerged the Nicene Creed. It officially declared Jesus a god (up to then he had been a mere man) and selected those writings, suitably edited and altered, that today we call the New Testament. The priests and bishops who disagreed were executed or banished. Constantine declared the new Christian creed to be law. Henceforth anybody who did not accept it was killed.

I think we have had enough of the "true-or-false" game. Let me tell you what I think the real story of Jesus was like.

Once upon a time at Nazareth, some years before 4 BC (Herod died in that year) a boy called Jesus was born. It was a normal and natural birth. In his youth he worked with his father, a carpenter. As he grew up he became interested in religion. He joined an honest and simple Jewish sect called "the Essene Brotherhood." He studied their beliefs and probably lived with them in their monastery for a few years.

When he was about 30 he felt he should apply what he had learned. For two years he journeyed from place to place, teaching and healing.

He had strong psychic power and was a very good healer. He was a medium, too, could hear spirit voices and see spirit inspirers, like many mediums and healers today. He had a strong personality and attracted many followers.

His outspoken remarks about the Church and the priests of his time made the authorities angry. They thought he was a dangerous nuisance. The Roman governor did not have too many soldiers available. He could not afford to have an agitator rousing the mob. He had to nip any revolt in the bud nice and early. Jesus looked a possible danger. So he was executed.

After his death his followers started to drift away. Then Paul came on the scene. He felt he must keep them together, so he told them Jesus was the Messiah the prophets had said would come and lead the Jews. Nothing was done to put the sayings of Jesus down in writing because they all thought the world was coming to an end very soon.

The story of Jesus was handed down by word of mouth. As always happens it was exaggerated. Thus his healing and spiritual acts were made into miracles.

In AD 70 Jerusalem fell. Many Jews then joined the new sect because it offered them hope that perhaps Jesus had been the leader they had awaited, and maybe they could restore the Jewish kingdom.

As the followers grew in number they began to feel they should look more important. So they adopted all the old ideas of the pagan gods, such as the virgin birth. After all, many gods before had enjoyed this prestige. They felt Jesus should have it, too.

Gradually the story of Jesus was written down. But what a story! After generations had told and retold it, his simple tale had been exaggerated, magnified and altered so that he himself could not have recognised it.

And then the sect attracted the men of Imperial Rome. Constantine was looking for a new religion. He declared it the state religion. A state religion had to have certain requirements. It could not be less than, say, Mithraism, which it replaced.

So the Council of Nicaea met to decide once and for all what Christianity, as it was now called, should contain. All the old stories, sayings and proverbs, the wonderful but untrue fables about Jesus were sorted out, edited and augmented; new bits were written in and made up.

37

From this came the New Testament more or less as we know it today. Jesus was declared a god. The Christian creed was written down. Anybody who did not believe exactly what had been written was killed. Christianity was born.

All religions started simply and in the same way. A man was born a natural psychic. He received a revelation. His spiritual awareness was very much greater than his fellows. The need to help his contemporaries to understand what had been denied them prompted him to share his knowledge. He became a teaching philosopher.

His revelation came from the spirit world. There, a step forward had been planned. Those who watch over our evolution arrange, from time to time, for us to receive a slightly wider awareness of their world. What they reveal is always more advanced than people of that period have so far been told. They choose a man as their instrument. Through him they reveal a little more of the divine pattern. Thus are we given regular opportunities to reorient our spiritual beliefs and to correct our philosophies.

Moses, Plato, Zoroaster, Buddha, Confucius, Socrates, Jesus and Mohammed are a few of the men who have been thus used. Since their message, in every case, came from the same source it has the same basic essentials. The revelation each received varied only in degree and presentation. It was, perhaps, different in so far as another race, civilisation or environment dictated. The spiritual awareness of the people at any one time and their ability to receive a revelation was the chief determining factor. What was disclosed was as much as people could accept in their state of evolution.

I have written "was," but should have written "is." I do not believe this is a process that has come to an end. It never will. We will progress. As we do so, other men will appear to show us the way. Our spiritual evolution is continuous.

It is my hope the day will surely come when the stranglehold of orthodoxy is released and the fresh air of spiritual truth is allowed freely to flow. For spiritual awareness is the birthright of all men. Without it our life here has no meaning or purpose.

Chapter Four

DEATH SHOULD NOT BE TABOO

THE Victorians covered their piano legs with little curtains. To them sex was something that was kept out of polite society. All legs should be covered. Sex was a taboo subject.

Today it is the exact opposite. Sex is written about, photographed, painted, discussed and used to sell anything from after-shave lotion to chicken chow mein. In fact sex is becoming a bore. But we still have our taboos. The current one is death.

People say, "If I should die . . ." They do not mean "if" but "when." Death comes to all of us. None can escape. One day your body will cease to function. Your heart will stop. The blood will no longer flow along veins and arteries.

The glands and body fluids will dry up. The computer that is your brain will be switched off. Putrefaction will set in very quickly. Your body will have to be burned or put in a deep hole and covered over. It is dead.

Most people fear death. This is understandable. The majority are brought up to accept the teachings of mainstream Christianity. They are told the Bible is true. It is the infallible word of God. The Bible tells them that if they are good they might go to heaven when they die—only "might," mind you, for many are called but few are chosen.

To become one of the few they have to join the right church, be baptised into the right faith, live their lives in accordance with a prescribed pattern and have their bodies buried in consecrated ground.

There are a lot of rules. It is terrifyingly easy to break a few. In fact it is impossible not to since just thinking about something you ought not to is considered as bad as doing it.

The alternative to going to heaven is to be sent to hell. There you face eternal damnation. If the worst fiendish torturer sat down and thought what could cause the most fear and dread he could not better eternal damnation. When your tooth aches, you can stand it if you know you are seeing the dentist tomorrow.

Women can put up with the pain and inconvenience of childbearing because they know it cannot last more than nine months. You can stand almost any pain, discomfort or torture if you know its duration. But if the suffering is to go on forever it becomes unbearable. Eternal means just that, for ever and ever.

If you do not accept the concept of going to heaven and living a beautiful life as an alternative to being tortured and in pain for ever after you die, then you may conclude that death is the end.

Many believe this. They say when the body dies they also do. Nothing survives except their memory in other men's minds. In time this too disappears. When the body is burned, or buried and eaten by worms, nothing remains. There is no soul, spirit, or surviving mind.

Death is the end.

This is almost as frightening. The idea that you as a person should one day be snuffed out like a candle flame cannot give anybody hope. If the end is death, nil, nothing, total annihilation, there is not much to live for. Why not become a hedonist? Live for pleasure. Eat, drink and be merry for tomorrow we die. Why not?

We know now both ideas are wrong. There is no heaven. There is no hell. There is no eternal damnation. The Bible is not God's word. It is the word of man, or rather of men using these terrible threats to control the minds of others.

Death is not the end. It is the beginning. It is a moment of change when you shrug off the body like an old overcoat you have been using. You are the butterfly emerging from the chrysalis. You enter a fuller, greater life.

There is no death. There is only life. And as you leave one form you utilise another. Life goes on. Your life goes on. The form might change, but you survive. You are immortal.

I believe a person's whole attitude to life is conditioned by his concept of death. If death means the high possibility of eternal damnation then there is the underlying fear of it. You may obey the rules, you may lead a "good life." You do so for the wrong reasons.

Fear is a hard taskmaster. The reward-and-punishment syndrome has kept people in chains for generations. You cannot live a full life on the basis of fear. You cannot obtain happiness and health on this diet. Nor can you on the basis of reward, on the satisfaction of being sure you will be chosen as one of the few to go to heaven. That smugness inhibits a full life almost as much as fear does.

What man can build, improve his mind, and enrich his life when he believes that in so short a time the total effort cannot avoid his feeding the worms?

I am sure unhappiness, stress, worry and most ill-health arise from this lack of understanding. You are immortal. You live for ever. You cannot die.

Accept this and everything changes. Nothing looks the same in the light of your immortality. You may have a problem at this minute. Look at it and think how unimportant it will seem in a hundred years' time. How unimportant will it seem in a few thousand years' time when you are living a full, interesting life in another world?

Think about death. Wipe out the taboo. Look at it. Laugh at it. It is a fraud, an empty threat, it does not exist. It is *life* that matters, your life. Resolve now, at this moment, to live it to the full.

The business of dying has got into the wrong hands, moved into the wrong environment and become a subject of dread to be spoken of in whispers.

When a man is very ill he generally appreciates rest and comfort, the security of his home, and those around him who are familiar and loved. Instead he is whisked out of his comfortable bed and on to a stretcher.

He goes into the ambulance for the mechanical rush across the city, with the two-tone hooter adding its banshee wail to the fear and discomfort. When he gets to hospital he is treated like a clinical experimental animal with no rights to an opinion or even to the knowledge of what is being done to him.

He is surrounded by people, often made even more impersonal in masks, and linked to machinery, pumps and electrical equipment. Samples of his blood and other fluids are drawn off.

He is surrounded by nurses, doctors, specialists, students, laboratory technicians, electronic experts and other frightening and unknown persons. He may be whisked off again to the radiography department where giant machines make him feel like a specimen on a slide.

Now he is treated as a thing. Decisions are made about him without his being consulted. He may end in the intensive care unit or the operating theatre. He will become the object of a great deal of technology and an immense amount of financial expenditure.

His fate may depend on a blood transfusion, a kidney machine, or major surgery. Those busy, masked figures who surround him may be interested in his pulse rate, blood content, urine, breathing or excretions. Not one is concerned with him as a human being.

If the poor man objects to all this activity, he will simply be sedated so there will be no more interference in the esoteric medical rituals. No time must be lost. Any consideration of a patient as a person wastes time. His life may well depend on ignoring him and his wishes. Death must be avoided regardless of the cost.

If the patient wants to die quietly in his own bed this wish cannot be expressed. If any decision is to be made it is done by the doctors or a relative. The horror of death and the unceasing efforts to avoid it are the primary directives. The patient's wishes or the quality of the life left to him are not considered.

The medical techniques may well succeed. A man who would have died a few years ago now lives. At the cost of a complete loss of dignity, perhaps considerable incapacitation, and certainly in the absence of any consideration for his own will, he is not allowed to die. He may be saved physically. Emotionally and spiritually the outcome may be considered differently.

Years ago, before the invention of anaesthesia and antibiotics, hospitals were regarded with horror by those who had to go into them. The mortality rate was very high. The pain and suffering were only marginally relieved. If you went to hospital your family were resigned to your death. If you emerged they knew you would never be the same again.

Today we are finding the same attitude towards hospitalisation. As a practising healer I do not see those who have been successfully treated. I get only the failures. Those who come to me do so after a long history of orthodox medical failure. Many are suffering as much from the "cures" as from the original disease.

I get patients with symptoms caused by drug therapy ranging from paralysis to blindness. I get patients who have been into hospital three or four or more times and have had a number of operations, none of which they can explain to me.

They have had nerves severed, organs removed, tubes and metal plates inserted. Many seem to have been used as experiments for guinea-pig surgery that has achieved nothing except to leave them painfully and permanently crippled.

I can find nothing in the training of medical doctors that equips them to make moral decisions. Whether a patient should live or die must be up to him, as must his understanding of the effect of the treatment that is given him and the quality of life that might remain.

I can find nothing in the training of medical doctors that equips them to deny a patient the knowledge of his impending death.

Death comes to us all. It is inevitable. It will happen to you. It will happen to me. There is no way you can avoid it. When your time comes you should have an opportunity of making ready for the great change you are to experience.

You deserve time and knowledge to enable you to be prepared mentally and spiritually for this great moment. And nobody has a right to deny you this.

A person who is near to death should have an opportunity to be in his own home, in his own bed, surrounded by those he loves and with the comfort and warmth of a well-known atmosphere. He should be able to talk to those who know the road he is going to travel, to get spiritual help and guidance, so that when the time comes to leave his now worn-out or damaged body he does so with dignity.

A person's death is the most important moment in his life. For his whole life has been a preparation for what is to follow. He is like a student who has come to the end of the course. Now he is ready to enter the great world outside the university backwater and to apply what he has learned. It is a moment that calls for care, consideration, understanding, compassion and love.

Death should not take place in the science-fiction environment of an intensive care unit or an operating theatre. Death is not a time for surgeons, doctors, laboratory technicians and nursing sisters in sterile gowns and masks.

Those of us who have sat with a dying individual and who have helped him to die know that it is not a time for horror. It is a time of peace and tranquillity. It is a moment when one soul can commune with another to help him on his way.

Because I am a spirit healer I often get brought to me patients who are suffering from the aftermath of grief. There are many symptoms, from colitis to partial paralysis. I have even met hysterical dumbness.

I listen with compassion to the stories they have to tell. It is surprising how often a similar picture is painted.

The passing of someone near is followed by a period of intense grief, and a longer time of formal mourning. The patient seems unable to recover his usual vigour. He finds he cannot sleep. He starts to have stress symptoms that every healer soon learns to recognise.

An analysis invariably reveals a guilt complex and an intense feeling of self-pity. The guilt is there because he knows of his omissions and weaknesses. Now that it is too late he can appreciate how much better his behaviour could have been. The self-pity manifests itself in grief, denial and the modern equivalent of sackcloth and ashes.

The pains, symptoms and sleeplessness are all psychosomatic. He does not need healing. He needs education.

When somebody close to you dies he goes to the next world. His life here, and the education it has provided him, is over. He enters upon a greater life and a higher education.

There are children who are afraid to leave school because it is a safe, secure and well known existence. The world of commerce, adults and manly responsibility is unknown and seems fraught with danger.

Yet the child must leave school. His education there is over. He has to pass on, perhaps to university, or a technical college, but certainly into the greatest school of all, that of practical experience.

You, too, will have to leave school one day. This world may be a poor one, but it is the one you understand and know. It gives you security. The next world is the unknown. The unknown is always a little fearful.

In the next world you review the life you led. You consider the mistakes you made and the benefits you gained by being aware of them. You sit in judgement on yourself.

You are surrounded by friends who love you. You are free of all pain and suffering, enjoying radiant health, mental tranquillity and a supreme sense of well-being. You look upon the world you have left, and what do you see?

Those who were close to you are crying and wailing. They are dressed in black. They beat their breasts. They are full of guilt and self-pity. They deny themselves any simple pleasure as a form of penitence.

You wonder at their ignorance and pity them. You are filled with compassion for their ignorance and stupidity. But you console yourself with the thought that one day you will be reunited. Then you will be able to explain it all to their poor, tortured minds.

It is not only wrong to mourn. It is both foolish and selfish.

> There is no Death!
>> What seems so is transition;
>> This life of mortal breath
>> Is but a suburb of the life elysian,
>> Whose portal we call Death.
>>> *Longfellow*

Chapter Five

SPIRITUALISM, PSYCHIC PHENOMENA AND MEDIUMSHIP

I DO not like "isms." People are too apt to tie labels on their attitudes and beliefs. I do not even like organised religion where you have to agree to beliefs and dogma without the opportunity of investigating them and deciding for yourself. If anybody asks me if I am a religious man, I must ask them to define "religious."

If being religious means going to a church or place of worship regularly, then I do not qualify. I never go. If being a religious man means I attach myself to some cult and agree with their dogma, then I am not a religious man. When I was asked this very question in a radio interview, I replied that my whole way of life was my religion.

There is nothing new in my philosophy. It was Dag Hammarskjold who summed it up very adequately when he wrote, "In the last analysis, it is our conception of death which decides our answers to all the questions that life puts to us."

If you believe death is the end and that the soul, assuming you think you have one, and the body and the mind are all completely finished at the moment of death, this must inhibit the way you look at life. There is no life after death, therefore there is no retribution, no answering for what you do, no heaven, no hell, no punishment, no reincarnation, no day of reckoning. Your only look out is to see that you are not caught by purely worldly material laws.

Of course, there are many who do not believe in survival of death, but who lead good lives and who behave well towards their fellows. This is because they know this makes for a better world and for a fuller life.

But the vast majority of people who do not believe in the existence of the human soul and in the survival of death behave in a manner that reflects this. They put themselves first. They try and get the most out of life. They welcome material things.

What other people believe and how they act must remain a uniquely personal responsibility. There is one person for whom I am fully responsible. That person is me.

I believe we are here as part of a process of spiritual evolution, that this life is an educational process (and perhaps a fairly elementary one at that). I believe we are all developing spiritually and that there are as many different levels and rates of development as there are people. I believe when we have finished with this life we go through a process of analysis. We sit in judgement on the life we have led and have to decide, maybe with some help from our guides, if we learned the lesson, or if we should come back and have another go.

Life is just like a course of education. We know when the course starts. We know what lectures and classes we should complete. We know when the holidays are. We know when the course comes to an end. This is pre-destination.

Within that framework we have free will. What we do on the course is up to us.

Spiritualism is defined by different people in different ways. But this is what it means to me. And if this definition is the right one, then call me a Spiritualist.

There is now a growing acceptance throughout the world that psychic phenomena not only exist, but seem to be at variance with orthodox scientific theory.

It was not so long ago that Uri Geller's ability to make broken watches work and bend cutlery and keys was the object of ridicule and suspicion.

Today we find young people following his exploits with similar results, and with little or no publicity. The "Geller effect" is now widely recognised and accepted.

It was not so long ago healers were classed with end-of-the-pier fortune-tellers and considered quacks and charlatans. Today doctors are referring more and more "incurable" patients to healers. Healing is being taught to nurses in hospitals.

The healer has not yet been fully accepted by the medical profession, but the opposition is crumbling in the face of the indisputable results that are obtained.

The ability of sensitives to forecast events, read minds, move inanimate objects, and communicate over vast distances by telepathy is not only now recognised, but is being researched in a number of countries.

There was at one time a hard school of scientific thought which maintained that if an effect was outside the rules of that science, then it must be false or one that had been inadequately controlled and investigated.

But at last scientists are realising their "rules" are nothing more than a conceit, that there are phenomena outside the scope of present scientific knowledge.

In his book "Lifetide," Lyall Watson tells of a small girl in Italy who could stroke a brand new tennis ball and persuade it to turn inside out. One moment the ball was in her hands with the fresh white furry outside showing. Then with a faint plop it turned inside out. The whole of the outside was now covered with black rubber.

Lyall Watson cut one ball open after she had done this and found not only that the white furry covering inside was intact, but that the air remained in the ball under pressure. She did it again. This time he kept the black rubber sphere on his desk to remind him of how inadequate was his ability to explain it.

If a young man can bend keys and spoons by rubbing them lightly, and start watches going again, and if a young girl can turn tennis balls inside out, it seems to me that what a healer does to the human body is in much the same category. The healing is a simple and effective demonstration of psychic power.

As a healer I find I get the most dramatic results with orthopedic disabilities. Slipped discs go back into place. Dislocated vertebrae return to their normal situations. Curved spines straighten.

I have never bothered much with bending spoons because straightening backs seems more important. But I am sure the ability to do these things is part of the same psychic function.

Some of the best scientific brains in the west are attempting to understand psychic phenomena. If you do not understand them do not scoff. Try to keep an open mind. And whatever you do avoid cynicism.

The main object of mediumship is to prove survival of death. There are people in this world who are born with the gift of mediumship.

If you have a natural gift you should develop it. The singer with perfect pitch, the painter with an innate sense of line and colour, the sculptor who can see the form enclosed in a block of stone, the composer whose mind is full of melody, all need to develop their techniques.

To become proficient in any field of artistic expression you need to take instruction, practise and develop technique. The same applies to mediumship. It takes dedication and self-control. It is too easy to misinterpret, distort and impose your own thoughts on those that flow through you.

A medium learns he is only an instrument, that he is being used by those in the spirit world who need him as a means of communication. The result of this dedicated application and humility is the flow of evidence through the medium that demonstrates to those who seek the truth the fact of survival of death.

Once you know you are immortal your whole philosophy must change. The way you live and think, your attitude to others, to material possessions, to life here as a whole, must undergo a radical change. It is natural to turn to spirit guides for help in reorientating your thinking. So we find that the secondary use of mediumship is the spread of spiritual philosophy.

That people seek comfort through mediumship is understandable. The removal of grief on the passing of one dear to you is a prerequisite to understanding that he survives. The trappings of death, the barbarism of funerals and the psychological bankruptcy of mourning have to be seen in a corrected perspective before a natural flow between those remaining here and the one who has passed on can be established.

Curiosity about life in the next world, the act of passing and the renewal of love with one you thought lost are natural. But once the novelty has worn off, once the fact of continued companionship can be accepted, mediumship can be seen to have performed its function.

We read much these days about the ways in which mediumship is being used for other ends. There is the businessman who sits regularly so he may get guidance to help him make even more money than the fortune he already enjoys.

There is the gambler who hopes to get the name of the winning horse. There are ordinary men and women who peer into the future. There are those who seek to solve crimes, to anticipate events, to find buried treasure, to learn something their fellows remain in ignorance about. All these are perversions of mediumship.

We all have guides. Each of us has one or more helpers in the spirit world who have chosen to guide us through this one. You do not need a medium to have them help you. If you remove all restrictive clothing, make yourself really comfortable, sit in your favourite chair, in a darkened, quiet room, and in this environment let your mind clear of its material thoughts, your guides will have the ideal conditions in which to communicate with you.

Maybe you will not hear voices or see visions. Maybe there will not be a magical change of light or a burning bush. You do not need them. Your guides work through a process of communion not communication. You will find you are soon getting help, guidance, comfort, support and all the answers you need.

We can all get help in this way. To seek to learn about the future through mediumship is to misuse a spiritual gift. There are many with a different gift. They have a sense extra to the ones you and I possess. This may enable them to look a little ahead, to warn you of pitfalls, to help you take the right road.

Palmists, fortune-tellers, crystal-gazers and "clairvoyants" are often not mediums. They have the extra perception that allows them to see a little further ahead than you can. There is no spirit direction. What they do is not a spiritual exercise.

You may find it interesting or even fun to visit them. But why should you wish to know the future? Most of us have not the spiritual strength correctly to live today. We cannot bear the burden of the future as well as we can that of the past. Many who come to me for healing are crucified between these two thieves, remorse for the past and fear for the future.

I believe most sincerely that true mediumship is one of the greatest gifts. It should not be prostituted. It should not be sacrificed on the twin altars of material greed and temporal curiosity. If your guides wish to communicate with you, they will do so. You have only to create the spiritual environment that facilitates this.

Mediumship is brought into disrepute by its application to functions other than the one for which it exists. I repeat with great conviction that the main object of mediumship is to prove survival. Following this comes the secondary function of the spread of spiritual philosophy.

The use of true mediumship for any other purpose is a perversion. In the end it can do no good for Spiritualism and for the understanding we seek to spread. Mediumship should be lifted from the crystal ball, tarot cards, cross-my-palm-with-silver image to be seen for what it is, one of the greatest gifts man can have.

Because a man is "dead" he is not automatically infallible. If a man was an interfering busybody in this life, then for a while at least he most probably will remain one in the next. After you make the great change we call "death" there is a period of adjustment. I do not know how long this period lasts. In any case, time in the next world is quite different from the way we know it in this one.

During the period of adjustment a man may still be emotionally connected with the earth. A miser who loved his wealth may take a lot of convincing he has left it irrevocably behind. Materialists generally find it hard to adjust to a spiritual life. So do those who have been brainwashed in any dogmatic beliefs.

Yet these are just the men who will wish to maintain their earthly connections, and, if they can, to communicate with us here. I am not suggesting for one moment that all who communicate through mediums are spiritually immature. Far from it.

Some are very evolved beings. Because this is their chosen task they have decided to stay on a plane that allows communication with us. There are many spiritually mature persons who wish for a while to remain in contact with people in this life, so they can do their part in helping and guiding and seeing that the great design is implemented.

Those who stay on a plane that enables them to do this because they wish it are in a special class. They are very much different from those who remain on a lower plane because that is where they belong for the moment, or because they are still so materially orientated they cannot rise above it.

I believe most hauntings (if not all of them) are caused by such persons. A medium is able to see, hear or feel their presence. A medium can commune or communicate and thus pick up and relay messages.

These messages may be merely the conveying of sentiments, a plea for release from the bondage that some form of materialism provides, or an effort to promote the unevolved philosophy that got them into this condition in the first place.

Thus, we must at all times keep in mind the nature of that person. If he was a meddler he may still be one. If he was wholly a materialist he may as yet be unable not to think in the same way. If he was selfish he will remain so for a time.

I remember a woman coming to me with a number of symptoms and asking for healing. They were all emotionally induced. The syndrome was of a person who had suffered a shock. Eventually she told me what had troubled her.

She was a Spiritualist and firmly accepted the fact of survival. She sat from time to time with a medium she knew. An aunt who had passed over a few years ago came through one evening. She said she would leave her house, sell it all up and go abroad within two years.

My patient made a number of preparations. Apart from the material arrangements there was the wrench of leaving the home she had learned to love. Three years later she was still living there. The invitation to go abroad had not materialised.

She was living in a vacuum waiting at any moment to pack up, sell up and get out. She was not getting any younger and the insecurity was the cause of her illness. She looked pleadingly at me. "Tell me how I should interpret that message," she said.

I asked about her aunt. She was a domineering woman who liked rearranging people's lives. I pointed out she was still trying to do just that. The interpretation of the message was simple, I told her. "She was wrong!"

Once I had convinced her a "dead" person is not automatically infallible, she changed. Her symptoms cleared up. She smiled and was there and then completely healed.

There must be many cases of people making themselves ill by trying to conform to spirit messages they have received from beings merely trying still to follow their earthly habits. By all means let us receive these messages. Listen to what any spirit person wishes to say. But remember they may be merely expressing an opinion—and they can be wrong.

Chapter Six

TODAY'S SEVEN DEADLY SINS

WHOEVER first listed the seven deadly sins was a sound psychiatrist. They are not sins against theology. They are sins against common sense. Any of them will make you ill. Any permutation of more than one will keep you ill. And any group of them can kill you. In case you cannot remember them all, they are pride, covetousness, lust, anger, gluttony, envy and sloth.

Pride. This is an "Overweening of one's own qualities," states the "Concise Oxford Dictionary."

Man is constantly torn between two vastly differing criteria. The standards that apply to his life here seem concerned with trivia by comparison with those of his immortality.

If a man is unaware of his survival of death, he knows only the one standard. His actions here are designed solely for personal gain or pleasure. Even if as a humanist he may feel responsibility towards his fellow-man, his responsibility is restricted to this world.

The qualities that a man enjoys stem from a natural gift, from an aptitude that has been developed, or from what appears to be a fortuitous set of circumstances. The man who is handsome may be proud of his appearance, yet he has done nothing to acquire his looks. The man who is brilliant may be proud of his mental capacity, yet it may be that he has merely inherited a high IQ. The musician may be proud of his compositions, yet the melodies may come into his head from an outside source.

Much of which we are proud is given to us. The ability to execute a great painting, to write a superb poem, or to compose fine music, may fill a man with pride. There are lesser accomplishments that have the same effect. A businessman may be proud of his acquired wealth, a woman of her cooking, a fashion model of her figure, an athlete of his body. What are you proud of?

For the gifts with which we are endowed we should be grateful. We had nothing to do with their giving; we merely received them. The accomplishments of which we are proud are concerned with our short life in this world. Perhaps another man with your opportunities, wealth, brain, imagination or education could have done so much better.

The dictionary defines pride as an "overweening" opinion. A craftsman has every right to be proud of a job well done, as long as he has humility for the gift of being able to do it. When he believes his skill, art, manual dexterity and sense of colour and form are not due to any outside influence, then his pride is wrong.

When a man "dies" and passes on to the next world, he reflects for a while in judgement of his earthly life. It unfolds like a television documentary. He can see clearly his faults, mistakes and omissions. There is no orthodox judgement day, heaven or hell. There is this cold, analytical self-appraisal that misses nothing because all is known.

Then the foolishness of pride can be seen. It is foolish because it denies the divinity of your gifts. It supposes that what you achieved was due to your unaided efforts. It denies the help you received from your guides. But worst of all it brings your accomplishments down to the level of the lower criterion.

Judge what you have done only by the measurements of this world and it may seem something to be proud about. Judge by the standards of immortality and it is insignificant. As Dryden said:

"My thoughtless youth was winged with vain desires,
My manhood, long misled by wandering fires,
Followed false lights; and when their glimpse was
    gone
My pride struck out new sparkles of her own.
Such was I, such by nature still I am;
Be Thine the glory, and be mine the shame!"

Covetousness. "Eagerly desirous of another's property, greed, avarice"—"Concise Oxford Dictionary."

There is a regular feature in a national newspaper that invariably makes me smile. It publishes a list of the amounts in people's wills under the heading, "Money They Left." Years of striving and scheming, a lifetime of small economies; or the elbowing aside of rivals, the battle of commerce, the ruthlessness of big business. The epitaph is a line in a column of figures—money they left.

Covetousness is the weakness of materialism. We live in a materialistic world. People are judged by their clothes, homes, cars and a host of carefully graded sta-

62

tus symbols. The successful man is the one who makes the most money. Stop 20 people in the street and ask them what they would like most to happen to them this week. Nineteen will ask to win the pools. The 20th will want something more specific.

If a man sees that by this standard a neighbour is more successful than he, then he wants what the man next door has. He prefers his neighbour's house, furniture, hi-fi and camera. If he had them he would not be happy.

The same standard would apply at a higher level. He would find a man who had more. Did he want a Rover? Now he knows a man who drives a Rolls. Did he want a detached house with a garden? Now he meets people who have several acres and a swimming pool.

There are always things better, bigger, shinier, newer, dearer, larger or a brighter pink than those you have. There will always be somebody who seems better-looking, better-dressed, better-endowed, having more fun and enjoying the material fruits of life more than you. Do not envy him.

Your life on earth is a short span in eternity. It is natural you want to make it pleasant and enjoyable. You cannot do this with things. You can do it only by attaining spiritual harmony.

Do not covet what your neighbour has. He probably has ulcers and high blood pressure as the price he had to pay. Do not covet your neighbour's wife. She may be a shrew. Perhaps his long hours at the office and the money he earns thereby is his method of avoiding a confrontation with her.

Do not covet anything. You can never know the

price a man paid to achieve it. There is an old Spanish proverb that goes, "Take what you want, says God, take it—and pay for it." Sometimes the price is too high. Often it is unnecessary, you do not need to make the purchase.

> "Thou shalt not covet thy neighbour's wife,
> nor his servant, nor his maid, nor his ox,
> nor his ass, nor any thing that is his"—The 10th
> Commandment

Lust. "Sensuous appetite regarded as sinful; animal desire for sexual indulgence, lascivious passion"— "Concise Oxford Dictionary."

I am often surprised there is not more honest lust about. We are subjected to persuasion on a scale never before experienced by civilised people. Advertising in the press, magazines, cinemas, on television and on hoardings, continually attracts us.

The most seen and heard basic ingredient is erotic stimulation. A provocative woman can sell anything from rolled steel joists on a manufacturer's calender to aftershave lotion with the promise of an aphrodisiac. Any magazine editor will tell you an erotically displayed female on the cover sells copies.

Do you go to the cinema because you are impressed by the producer's artistic attributes or by the busty blonde on the hoardings? Even children's comics are full of tightly-clothed nymphets.

It seems to me we men are exercising great restraint despite constant stimulation. I think we have our lust well in check. I am uncertain whether it is checked by opportunity or by maturity.

Perhaps the fact we live in a cold climate, that most girls are indoors at home a lot, that love and passion are difficult in the cold and rain, and that for the best part of the year we are all muffled up, tend to make us better behaved.

We do have sensuous appetites, most of us. This is just as well for the continuation of the human race. But as we mature we realise the enjoyment of our appetites is greater if we are selective. The man who is sated will produce little.

The great painters, inventors, poets and composers, the men who make their mark in art, politics, the theatre and in the humanities, are often men who have diverted their sex urge into other channels.

The free indulgence of our appetites does not contribute towards spiritual maturity. Nor does enforced celibacy. The golden rule is moderation in all things.

> "But at my back I always hear
> Time's winged chariot hurrying near.
> And yonder all before us lie
> Deserts of vast eternity.
> Thy beauty shall no more be found;
> Nor, in thy marble vault, shall sound
> My echoing song: then worms shall try
> That long preserved virginity:
> And your quaint honour turn to dust;
> And into ashes all my lust"—Andrew Marvell.

Anger. "Rage, hot displeasure"—"Concise Oxford Dictionary."

The "sin" of anger is the mistake of losing your temper. Perhaps I should have dealt with the word "sin" a lot earlier. I do not accept the Church's teachings as infallible. Therefore, I cannot bow to a "divine law" which I know to have been of man's creation. A sin is a transgression against this law.

Instead I believe in the principle of personal responsibility. The rightness or wrongness of any action of yours is determined by the stage of spiritual evolution you have reached at that time. If, for instance, a cannibal eats his enemy it may not be wrong. The savage has been brought up to eat human flesh. He is not sufficiently spiritually evolved to know it is wrong.

He cannot be blamed. But you know. You have reached that stage. You do not eat your fellow-men. But perhaps you eat animals. Another person will have evolved further spiritually than you have. He will know it is wrong to kill and to eat living animals. He has become a vegetarian. If you eat a piece of a cow it may not be wrong for you. It would be very wrong for a vegetarian.

Your personal degree of spiritual awareness is the only criterion of the rightness of your own actions.

On a number of points the philosophers, who were responsible for the world's "holy books," recommended behaviour that is remarkably consistent with that postulated by psychiatrists.

They agree, for instance, about anger. If you lose your temper your body undergoes changes. Your blood pressure goes up, your pulse and heart beat increase, your blood multiplies its ability to clot. The adrenalin that is pumped into your bloodstream is the main trigger substance for a very quick change in the whole metabolism of your body.

66

When your temper dies and your body mechanism returns to normal, you can assess the risks. High blood pressure is dangerous; pressure on your arteries is dangerous. These can cause death. If you go on losing your temper too often they will. Turning the other cheek is not only a good philosophy but good medicine.

If you find it hard at first to produce the soft answer that turneth away wrath, then try instead to assess the damage anger causes. It is not damage to the one you are angry with. It is damage to you. The man who dies in middle-age from a coronary thrombosis, a stroke, or heart failure, may well be the victim of his own anger.

Anger is not a sin any more. It is downright stupidity.

"Anger's my meat; I sup upon myself,
    And so shall starve with feeding"—Shakespeare.

Glutton. "Excessive eating, gormandising"—"Concise Oxford Dictionary."

While one half of the world starves, the other half eats too much. Most of the western world is guilty of gluttony. On the altar of this false god are sacrificed hundreds of thousands of animals every day.

Never has the sacrifice of living creatures achieved such enormous proportions. Broiler houses, where hens are reared under factory conditions, produce a constant supply of dead bodies. Chickens, pigs, calves, rabbits, bullocks, sheep, lambs, cows, turkeys, pheasants, ducks, geese, the list seems endless. These are the living sacrifices on the altar of gluttony.

To produce vegetables and fruit in great quantities means the extermination of the slightest opposition.

The chemicals used destroy many forms of life. Birds, small animals and insects are poisoned by sprays. How much of these substances find their way into human bodies cannot be calculated.

The slaughterhouses reek with blood and fear as terrified animals face death. Stunned, its brain ripped out, its proud body slung up on hooks, a once lovely animal that lived, moved and had sensations is cut into pieces.

These are quick-frozen. Months or years later they are thawed. The red colour is due to dye injection; the flavour is restored by chemicals; the cellular structure is broken down by other chemicals to produce a tender, juicy, red steak.

It is my conviction that with spiritual maturity comes the knowledge of what is acceptable as a diet. I believe every evolved Spiritualist must eventually become a vegetarian and live on a simple diet of unprocessed, fresh natural foods. The sin of gluttony is abhorrent to a mature person. It is probably the biggest indictment of civilisation. We should be ashamed of our diet.

With a change of dietary habits, and a release from ritual murder of the animal world, would come a rising standard of spiritual awareness. Gradually, too, would the world distribution of food adjust itself as the needs of the west became more modest.

There is nothing to be said for gluttony. It is without a single exonerating fact. The death of gluttony would bring life to thousands upon thousands who would otherwise starve. To send money to starving nations while we indulge in gluttony is an affront to human dignity. We must call for a world revision of eating habits. The word "sin" is indeed an old-fashioned one.

In this respect maybe it is the best word, for gluttony is a deadly sin.

"I believe that where the love of God is verily perfected, and the true spirit of government watchfully attended to, a tenderness towards all creatures made subject to us will be experienced, and a care felt in us that we do not lessen that sweetness of life in the animal creation which the Great Creator intends for them under our government"—John Woolman.

Envy. "Grudging contemplation of more fortunate persons"—"Concise Oxford Dictionary."

Envy is green, the correct colour. For envy is rotten and corroding. It does not harm the man who is envied. It rots the man who envies.

It is inevitable in any society some men have more than others. The dream of complete equality is a false one. It denies that men are born at different stages of their spiritual evolution and with different bodily and mental equipment. Equality of opportunity may one day be possible. But what you do with your opportunities depends on your health, bodily efficiency, mental capacity, imagination and the degree of spiritual awareness that is vouchsafed you.

One may have a fine body and a clear mind. Yet he may be so poorly evolved spiritually he enjoys juicy steaks, gives vent to his lusts, is indifferent to human and animal suffering, does not believe in the sanctity of life and has no thought for the next world.

Another may be crippled and ugly, be born into poverty, and perhaps lack in an important attribute, such as hearing or vision. Yet he may be spiritually mature, have a great reverence for life and contribute enormously to the general fund of goodness.

Envy is foolish. You can only envy the things you can see a man has. These are material or superficial possessions. You cannot know the price he paid, or whether in similar circumstances you would do so. Each must decide his needs and set his priorities. If you need material success you must work for it. Envying another man's will not bring your success.

There are two ways to get to the top of the tree. One is to climb it. The other is to sit on an acorn and wait. While you are sitting there you have no right to envy the man who has found a tree and climbed to the top.

Envy is corrosive. It is one of those feelings that seeps into the mind. It colours our actions, distorts our thoughts and ruins our bodies. Most of the ills of modern life are emotionally induced. Envy induces illness.

The pain and the suffering are real, not imaginary. But the cause is not functional. It is the malfunction of your body because you have upset its harmony.

The symptoms of diseases actuated by envy are well known. The list reads like a textbook of psychosomatic medicine. Over 50 per cent of patients attending hospital clinics are suffering from emotionally-induced illness. I am not referring to those who visit a doctor, but patients who have such severe symptoms they are sent to hospital.

Look at this figure again. It means that if a medical student in that hospital opened a book of the hundred most prevalent diseases, emotionally-induced illness would appear as often as the other 99 put together. I have no statistics about envy, but it is a main contributory factor in this type of complaint.

The degree of man's envy is the measure of his spiritual immaturity. It is physically corrosive. The quicker you grow up the longer you will live.

> "The internal serpent; he it was, whose guile,
> Stirr'd up with envy and revenge, deceived
> The mother of mankind"—Milton.

Sloth. "Laziness, indolence"—"Concise Oxford Dictionary."

It is natural and right for a man to work. We seldom, in the course of a normal span of years, fully utilise either our mental or physical potential. The brain is a remarkable computer. It is even now only dimly understood.

There is no doubt most of us use only a small part of its capabilities. Once a method is adopted of programming a human brain we shall be able to assimilate an enormous amount of knowledge and apply it. The human brain is controlled by a mind that is unique. It has imagination.

The human body is the most complex, perfect machine we know. Nothing man has invented or constructed comes anywhere near its beauty, complexity and efficiency. We have hardly started to develop it. Occasionally a lifetime of total dedication, allied to a natural gift, will demonstrate just how far development can go. Nobody who has seen and listened to a great concert pianist can doubt this claim.

The human body, mind and brain, and the spirit that inhabits this frame, need the stimulation of a short-term and a long-term objective. These are supplied by work, hobbies, voluntary activities, sports, mixing with other people and stimulation of a common task.

The man with a mind full of ideas must pass them on. The artist must paint, the author must write, the musician must play, the composer must produce music, the singer must sing, and you, my friend, whatever you can do you must do.

Laziness, indolence and sloth are the denigration of progress, the denial of fulfilment and the enemies of personal happiness. The man whose ideal life is to laze for ever on a South Sea island beach is a fool. He will awaken one day and find he has lazed his life away. When he reaches the next world, and looks back on his life in this one, his judgement on his actions will be to shake his head and mutter, "What a waste, what a waste!"

Sloth can never bring happiness. It brings only a lack of satisfaction, emptiness and an ultimate sense of futility.

> "Awake my soul, and with the sun
> Thy daily stage of duty run;
> Shake off dull sloth, and joyful rise
> To pay thy morning sacrifice"—Morning hymn.

Chapter Seven

HERE'S HEALTH

MORE than half the patients who come to me need education rather than healing. The ailments which are regularly paraded are often the result of wrong living, wrong thinking, wrong diet and wrong attitudes.

It is not my function to educate people. I am a healer. My job is to heal the sick. But I do appreciate healing is a means and not an end in itself. Through it, a person becomes aware of his spiritual life.

When a man is healed of a disease that has proved medically incurable he is never quite the same again. He must want to know more of the forces that made him well. I can show him where to find out about spiritual matters. I can tell him what books to read. I can discuss his problems and guide him towards the right road.

But he must have the desire to travel that road. The seeds of that wish are planted when the healing takes place. Thus the healing comes first—and the spiritual awareness follows.

Yet so many patients these days are not suffering from functional diseases. The ailments they bring to me are either psychosomatically induced or the results of sheer ignorance in the science of living, or both.

The acts of eating and drinking now fulfil many functions. We eat as a social convention. Hostesses take a lot of trouble to make their dinners a great success. We eat in order to satisfy our taste for sensuality.

Chefs vie with one another to produce better and more subtle variations of a dish. We eat as a substitute for some psychological need. Compulsive eaters prove this.

We eat as an adventure. We try new foods and foreign concoctions.

We drink also as a social convention. Around the consumption of a drug called alcohol we have erected a whole edifice of social conventions.

"This is my round," we say, or "One for the road," "Have this one on me," "Let's have some people in for drinks."

Non-alcoholic drinks have their conventions too. The morning cup of coffee has become almost as necessary a ritual as the tea ceremony. And even soft drinks have their addicts and conventions like "the pause that refreshes."

Eating and drinking have one important function that has for long been overlooked. They fuel the body. You may consider fuel as simple intake of energy. It is more complex.

Even your car needs more than just petrol. It needs one of a certain octane rating. It requires one type of oil for the sump, another for the gear box, and a third for the back axle.

A car must have grease for the chassis, special fluid for the hydraulic brakes and clutch, ordinary water for the radiator, and one that has been distilled for the battery.

Put the wrong fuel in the wrong place and you are in trouble. This may be obvious if you put distilled water in the sump and sump oil in the battery.

Your body is a far more complex mechanism than any motor car. It demands a wide variety of fuels.

Fuelling the body intelligently is of paramount importance in the search for health. We are the largest consumer of refined white sugar in the world. It is no coincidence we also have the largest incidence of arthritis. They are linked.

Stomach disorders are connected with the massive consumption of white bread and white refined flour. The bran, bulk, wheat germ and virtually all the goodness that bread once held has now been eliminated.

Bread today is a factory product. It is white, steamed dough, treated with chalk to make it whiter and with chemicals to ensure longer freshness.

The huge consumption of factory-processed food is a prime cause of disease. All the vitamins, amino acids, trace elements and the real goodness are removed in the complex process.

Dyes are added to give the right colour. Chemicals are introduced to provide the acceptable taste, smell and consistency.

The final product may look and taste good. It certainly will be easy to prepare. But it will not contribute towards your good.

Breakfast cereals are consumed by the ton every morning. Mothers send their families to work and to school in the happy belief they have been well fed.

There is more nutrient in the cardboard of the packet than in the content of most cereals. The processing so removes all food values that some manufacturers add artificial vitamins to provide some nutriment.

Instant mashed potatoes are in the same category. The potato provides a source of Vitamin C in winter. Instant potatoes have all the vitamins processed out of them.

Because a mother refuses to breast feed her baby on grounds of convenience, the preservation of her figure, or some other feminine selfishness, the baby is fed on cow's milk. The cow has eaten grass treated with insecticides growing from ground with a high Strontium 90 absorbtion. The cow is treated with hormones and other drugs to increase milk yield. How many potentially harmful chemicals the baby digests is difficult to assess. From babyhood onwards our diet is degraded.

Twentieth-century man gives more consideration to the quality of the petrol he puts into his car than to the food he puts in his stomach.

Health is a talent. There are diseases and disabilities that are congenital. But these are the exceptions. Most sick people are the architects of their own illness.

To get yourself well, and to maintain abounding good health, call for a total dedication to these ends. It may mean altering your diet, philosophy, attitudes and entire life style. Only you can decide if it is worth it.

Often sick people who come to me for healing say, "I would give anything to be well." Very few mean it. If a person is willing to give up smoking, alcohol, meat, processed food, sugar, white bread and flour products, and live on a regimen of fresh natural products such as fruit, vegetables, pulses and cereals, he will soon start to feel a lot better.

If he gives up tea and coffee and drinks only mineral water, his system will become cleansed of the accumulation of impurities he has been storing for years. He will then have to change his daily habits and make sure he walks two or three miles a day, gives up using a car or bus in favour of exercise, and spends much more time out of doors in an occupation such as gardening.

Since emotions are a primary cause of illness he will have to change his attitudes to life, to adopt a new philosophy and to acquire a degree of emotional stability.

All this takes time, effort and dedication. Only you can decide if it is worth while. Only you can put a value on good health.

When I discovered something quite new about human behaviour and health I felt elated. The things I found out I included in my book, "How to be Healthy, Wealthy and Wise." It has been widely read and well received. But now I know there is nothing completely new in its pages. Perhaps, there never is. My discoveries about human behaviour have been noted before. But they were new to me. And they provided some food for thought for many readers. Let me tell you about it.

People who are ill appear in two distinct categories. Regardless of their deformities, their pains and the sheer inconvenience of their diseases, they fall into one of these two groups. Either they enjoy life or they do not. Those who enjoy life generally get well. Those who do not seldom do. That is unless their coming to me reorientates their thinking.

As a healer I have no preknowledge of who will get better or who will not. But I try to give my patients the fullest opportunity to respond to the healing they receive through me. This I do by revealing the discovery I have made.

Your bodily control mechanism reacts to your attitude. If you are angry your pulse rate goes up, your blood pressure increases, adrenalin is pumped into your bloodstream; your blood increases its ability to clot in case you are wounded, your muscles tense, your whole body is made ready to spring into action to fight, to defend, to run.

When you are afraid similar chain reactions are triggered. You perspire, your throat goes dry, you may even have temporary paralysis. Nothing physical happens to you. It was your attitude that triggered off the whole reaction. And it was your change of attitude, one of relief, that told your defences to stand down.

It is your attitude alone that controls your body's reactions. And here was my discovery. You can control your body by an artificially induced attitude even if you know it to be false. As anger and fear produce strain and illness, so do happiness and optimism induce health and tranquillity. If, therefore, instead of being fearful and miserable you show all the symptoms of confidence and happiness, your body will adjust itself to these attitudes, even if in your mind you know them to be false and purposely simulated.

Try it. Now, at this instant, stop whatever you are doing. Pause. Decide for one hour only you will exhibit all the symptoms of a supremely happy person. Smile, laugh, sing, tell everybody you feel fine, it is a lovely day, the world is a wonderful place and that you have never felt happier. Do this for one hour.

Never mind if you do not believe it. Adopt this attitude. Your body's control mechanism will react. It will say to itself: "He is happy and well, he does not need more blood pressure, more oxygen, more adrenalin, more acid, more defences. He is well and happy. I will stop over-making all these chemicals and restore the balance of the body." And so it will.

In one hour you will feel fine. In a very short while this therapy will convert the imbalance that is making you ill into a harmony that keeps you well.

It is your attitude that controls your body. You can change the picture from misery and disease to happiness and health by altering your attitude, even if initially you know it to be simulated.

This was my discovery. It has changed the lives of many. It will work for you. Try it now.

This is a sick world. Ask any doctor, any healer or look at the statistics of sickness, disabilities, terminal diseases and commercial and industrial absenteeism. Not only are we suffering from physical sickness, but there is also an epidemic in the western world of spiritual ailments.

The time is ripe for a spiritual revival. God knows, we need one right now. Selfishness, greed, the lust for power, the target of personal gain irrespective of the cost, these are the symptoms of this ailment.

Many illnesses respond to old-fashioned remedies. Let me list some that may cure the sickness from which our society now suffers.

The first, and perhaps the most important initial step we can take, is to re-establish the home and the family as an essential social and economical unit. The words "home" and "family" should be indivisible. Home is a sharing, loving and working unit. It is the lowest social and economic unit in the national scale. Yet it is the most important.

Home is where mother and father bring up children in a harmonious atmosphere, where they feel a sense of belonging, where everybody in the family is secure, wanted and loved.

The most powerful way of influencing children is by example. Home is the place where you demonstrate how to live, how to cope with problems, how to share pleasures and pain and where you can see the magnificent power of love at work.

The second precept is to teach your children always to do their best and to show them by your own example just how to do this. It is right that at some time you ask for help. You can ask your parents, brothers or sisters for help. You can ask your friends or professional associates for help. It is right that you do so. You can ask God, whatever you conceive Him to be, for help. But only after you have done your very best and you are satisfied in your heart that this is so.

"Ask and ye shall receive." This is true. But you have to become receptive. And the way to do this is to do your very best in any circumstances. If you have a task to perform invariably do it as well as you can. Try and stand on your own two feet. Work at it. Then, and only then, ask for help. For then and only then have you put yourself in a position to receive it.

There is a symptom of the social and spiritual sickness that engulfs all levels of society. This is the assumption that work is a drudge. There are people who would rather accept national assistance money than work.

There are trade unions that ask for earlier retirement. There are thousands of people who get up every morning and hate the idea of going to work. How wrong they are!

Hard work is good for you. Early retirement brings early death. This is not a theory. There is ample statistical proof. There is no way any man or woman can live a full, happy life in idleness. It is just not possible. We need to work. We need to be fully, gainfully and interestingly occupied. Work is an essential element to a full and long life.

You may be doing a job you hate. That is bad for you.

Change your attitude or change your job. You may not find this easy. Why should it be? Anything that is too easy is probably not worth doing, anyhow. You may find that the new job pays less. No matter. Find a job you like and enjoy—and the rewards will be immeasurable.

These are simple, well-tried methods. You may even say they are old-fashioned. Perhaps they are. Perhaps all great truths are old. There is nothing new. Everything has been known before. But these rules of living have been forgotten and the sickness of society is the proof.

If there is a common denominator among the sick who come to me for healing it is that most of them are muddled thinkers. They are not fools, nor are they uneducated.

My patients are a good, representative, cross-section of the community. Some are educated to a high standard. Many are well read. All have the knowledge and ability to analyse their troubles. None of them do.

One of the most common muddles is about prayer. People think that if they pray hard enough, in the right manner and in the correct place, God will listen. He will see where He was unjust, where He went wrong and who deserves better treatment than He meted out. He will then reorganise things so you win the football pools, enjoy robust health and have all your problems solved. This is rubbish.

God plays no favourites. You have an equal opportunity with everybody else to draw on the enormous power available. What you do with it is up to you.

Another example of muddled thinking is that ill-health is a punishment for something. Patients feel guilt. They think their aches, pains and disabilities are there because they have done something wrong and are being punished. This, too, is utter nonsense.

You have free will. The way you behave is up to you. If you think and act at all times in accordance with the Golden Rule, if you abstain from bodily and mental perversions, then you will be well and bounding with health. You have a free choice. You punish yourself when you go against the natural laws and principles.

Any fool can profit from his successes. It takes a wise man to profit from his losses. We all make mistakes. From these we learn. Practise looking for the lesson. Whenever anything happens which you regard as a bad thing, look for the good. Look for the lesson this teaches you. It is a part of the university of evolution we call life.

For your life here is merely that, an education. You know when it starts. The end of term is also known. So is the syllabus. What you do, the lessons you learn, your behaviour here and the extent to which you benefit by the course—like that at any other college—is up to you.

Again like any other course, from time to time you have examinations or tests to see how you are getting on. The experiences you have, and the problems you must face, comprise these tests.

Try and meet them constructively. When you have met them philosophically you will see the good they do, not only to you, but also to the people around you.

Get out of the habit of blaming outside circumstances for the things that do not happen to you. Do not seek an alibi. A disability is there to be overcome. A weakness has been given you to see how you cope with it. Turn every disadvantage to an advantage. Develop your ability to link with the great power around you to overcome it.

The price you have to pay to earn your share of the health, wealth and happiness waiting for you in this world is the effort to control your attitude, thinking and actions so that they comply with the spiritual philosophy common to all great religious teachers.

Resolve today, now, to go forward and never to look back. Be optimistic at all times. Replace negative thoughts with positive ones. Fear nothing. Supplant worry with faith. Never surrender to despair or discouragement. Live each day to the full. Learn to draw on the great power available to you.

Are you carrying a burden? Does it seem too heavy? It is probably three times heavier than it need be!

Imagine you have a pack on your back. It is a great weight. You have to carry it a long way. It is becoming too much for you. Then you meet a man who stands in your path and laughs at your discomfort.

He examines your load and quickly shows you that two-thirds of it is unnecessary packaging material. He helps you discard it. Then when you lift the now-lightened burden on your shoulders again, he shows you the road is much shorter than you imagined. You thought it was many miles. It is only a few yards.

With a burden only one-third its previous weight, and a journey much shorter than you anticipated, you go on your way whistling.

I am the man. This is our meeting. Stop! Put down your load. Let us look at it together.

Part of the weight you carry is the past. Remorse, regret, sadness, longing and guilt for the past. Throw it out. Forget it. Listen to Carl Sandberg when he says, "I tell you the past is a bucket of ashes." Nothing you can do can alter anything in the past. It is finished, done with, over—throw it out!

Dry your eyes, put aside your remorse, stop blaming yourself.

Feeling better? Of course you are. Your load is already one-third lighter.

Let us examine it again. You are over-concerned for the future. You worry about what might happen to you. To your money, to your family. You are filled with apprehension. Throw it out!

The future is not here yet. When it arrives we will deal with it. Until then listen to the words of Albert Einstein. He was a clever man. He said: "I never think of the future. It comes soon enough." Yet Einstein was only repeating what many men had said many times before.

We find in Matthew VI, 34: "Take therefore no thought for the morrow; for the morrow shall take thought for the things of itself."

I am convinced the things we worry about most never happen. You may die in your sleep tonight. There may be no tomorrow. If it does come it could be radiant with hope, happiness and fulfilment. When it comes, deal with it. Until then do not think of it. Cast out fear, apprehension, worry, dread.

That is two-thirds of your burden gone. The load that is left is light and easy to bear. All you have to carry is the present.

What about the road ahead? Is it not a long one? No, it is short, very short. Let me show you. Your journey stops tonight. All you have to do is to carry the burden of the present for one day only.

Tomorrow does not yet exist. Tomorrow you may be in the next world. Tomorrow never comes. Today is all that there is. Until today ends, that is the length of your road.

When you awake in the morning thank God for today. Resolve to do your best with it. When it is over, give thanks again for it. Forget it and go to sleep.

This philosophy has been recognised by many men. It was Franklin who said, "One today is worth two tomorrows." More positively Martial wrote, "Tomorrow life is too late: live today." But the one I favour is even more direct, "Trust God and live one day at a time."

Your road is short. Your burden is only a third of what it was. Step out with a light heart. Today you met a man who lightened your load and shortened your journey.

It has been my privilege.

Chapter Eight

YOUR LIFE IS A PICTURE ONLY YOU CAN PAINT

THE basic difference between the mental process of an artist and that of a critic is his ability to anticipate. The critic looks at the picture. He tries to visualise the original scene. He makes an assessment of the way the artist saw it and the technique he used to transfer it onto canvas.

But the artist anticipated the picture. It was there in his mind's eye. His technique was merely a method of recording what already existed.

A man who cannot anticipate the finished picture, and who does not possess the technique to record it, may still retain his faculties of appreciation.

A man's life is a picture. Everything that happens to you draws another line. The lessons that failures teach add another touch of colour. The services you render, the happiness you spread, the laughter, love, compassion and understanding, they are all there, golden, silver and white.

The intolerance, greed, lust, gluttony, envy and ill-will, they are there, too, green, grey and black. Some of your picture shows already, in your manner, through your reactions, and on your face.

At 20 you have the face God gave you. At 40 you have the face you gave yourself.

When his picture is completed the artist steps back so that he may appraise his labour. It is his life's work — this picture of his existence. He steps out of our world. He sheds the artist's smock, the body he has worn. He takes a long, searching look at what he has completed.

His guides welcome him. They are his critics. They look at the picture that was his life. But he is the most critical of them all because only he knows how much better he could have done.

In time this will happen to you. When your earthly span is over your body will be discarded. You will leave this world. But before your spiritual evolution can continue there will be this moment of appraisal. You cannot avoid it. Your life here is going to be criticised, action by action, brush stroke by brush stroke. It will be examined in broad canvas and in the minutest detail.

When you divest yourself of your earthly body you also cast off the costume, the make-up and the props of the part you have played. The real you emerges, the distilled essence of you, the spiritual you. You are free of the role and the prejudices, ignorance and short-sightedness.

Now you can see it all, not only the picture, but the frame. You see not only the brush strokes but the motivations. You see not only the colours but the form.

Although every artist knows he will take a final truthful look at his work, he takes every opportunity of evaluating what he is doing during its progress. Watch him in his studio. He will pause, take a few steps back, cock his head on one side.

Suddenly he will pack up, clean off his palette, put his brushes away and leave it all for a couple of days. When he starts again, the eye is fresh, his inspiration is renewed.

You, too, can appraise, adjust and amend your life's work as it progresses. Why wait until it is finished? Step back a few paces. Take a long, critical look at what you are creating.

The essential ingredients that make a successful work of life have been defined by many philosophers and religious leaders. Among them are unselfishness, service, love, compassion, spiritual appreciation of truth, righteousness and survival of the human soul.

In art circles a man may remain a critic. He need never paint a picture, yet he may become an authority. In the world that we now know this is not possible. Each one of us is producing the picture of his life. You create now and criticise later.

You know what will be the basis of criticism. What you do not know is when the picture will be finished. Your life here may end tomorrow. It may take several more decades. Therefore you must proceed on the assumption that your workmanship will stand up to inspection at any time.

You may not have the opportunity of finishing or improving your work. When the time comes for you to go to the next world, will you look back on your life here with affection? Could you say, "The world is now a better place because of me"? Will you look lovingly at the broad canvas you have painted and feel you did your best?

Perhaps when you know you can do no more you will feel remorse for the poor picture you have painted. You may say: "Let me stay a little longer, let me scrape the canvas clean and start again. I am sure I can do better."

But the canvas is dry, the palette is clean, the brushes have been put away, the paint-flecked, worn smock has been discarded. It is done.

Few of us can produce masterpieces. All of us are capable of turning out a sound piece of work that is the very best that we can do with what we have.

Will your life's work stand the test?

Appendix

CANCER: CAN IT BE HEALED—AND CAN IT BE PREVENTED?

LET us say it aloud. *Cancer.*

Most people whisper it to me. Some will not even let the dreaded word pass their lips. They talk about a tumour, or use some other medical term. Some whisper "Big C." So let us get it out into the open and talk about it.

If it was catching the authorities would have classified it as an epidemic by now.

It is one of the most common diseases with which a healer has to deal. There is probably not a household in Britain where they do not know of somebody who has cancer or who has died of it.

One woman in 18 in this country develops breast cancer. It is a widespread cause of death throughout the western world.

I am told the total amount collected by cancer research funds now totals over £70,000,000 a year. Yet they are no nearer to finding a cure, and certainly no nearer to preventing it.

The standard medical or surgical treatment for cancer is barbaric.

There are three main treatments. These are surgery, when the cancer is cut away and parts of the patient cut off and thrown away too. You find women who have had their breasts removed, young people who have had a leg amputated, and men without a number of what we might naively assume were essential internal organs.

Allied to surgery is ray treatment. Here the patient is subjected to strong doses of X-rays that kill off the cells.

It seems a simple enough process, but the results I have seen can produce suppurating sores over the entire body, swelling of the joints, making walking impossible, sickness, vertigo, a lowering of vitality and the will to live.

The third treatment is chemotherapy. This is a method of killing the cells by getting the patient to take massive doses of powerful chemicals.

Apart from upsetting the delicate balance of the body this treatment often results in sickness, vomiting, vertigo, and a feeling of deep depression.

In addition the patient's hair falls out and he or she looks terrible.

I do appreciate a healer only sees the failures. There may well be men and women who respond well to these drastic treatments. I have seen none. The ones who come to me seem to be victims rather than patients.

Many have had all three treatments. The prognosis is still poor. Their life expectancy is only a few months.

I have never met a man or a woman who has had cancer, undergone the conventional treatment and not regretted it. But, as I say, I get only the failures.

It is worth remarking, however, that not one penny of the £70,000,000 collected by cancer research funds has been allocated to spiritual healing.

So what can a healer do? The most promising thing is he can teach people preventive medicine.

The cells in our bodies renew themselves on a continuing basis throughout our lives. There is not one cell in your body that was there ten years ago.

The cells regenerate in the precise form of the original. It is when they fail to do this you get "wild" cells which spread throughout the body. This is the disease we call "cancer."

But note the word "disease." Split it up into two. You get "dis" and "ease." It is this lack of ease, this lack of serenity and tranquillity, that is the basic cause of cancer.

It is my considered opinion cancer is triggered by stress. I do not believe stress alone is the cause. A bad diet, heavy smoking and a polluted environment play their part. But the trigger is stress.

As long as 30 years ago a Scottish doctor named Kissen did some personal research into the type of man who contracted lung cancer. His research was restricted to male heavy smokers, so that in theory they were all at risk.

However, he found the men who did get lung cancer were the ones who let stress build up inside them. They might not have showed it externally, but it was there. Dr Kissen described it as 'bottling up" their stress.

In America, at about the same time, Dr William Greene found that strong emotional stress was a fairly common factor in patients who contracted leukemia, cancer of the blood.

It is now an accepted medical fact cancer is triggered by stress. In particular breast cancer in women is prevalent in those who suppress their emotions. In other words, the "bottling up" attitude that Dr Kissen found in male smokers with lung cancer is common to women with breast cancer.

Anger, bottling up emotions and similar reactions to modern living make the body produce extra quantities of Immunoglobin A, which is manufactured in the breast itself. This condition is one found most often in breast cancer.

There are other chemical reactions in the body which inhibit the regeneration of normal healthy cells. These extra chemicals are triggered by stress.

It follows, therefore, that if a man or a woman can adopt a serene and tranquil attitude the risk of getting cancer is very small indeed.

The attitude that produces this lack of reaction to stress is the measure of our spiritual maturity.

It is perhaps an indicator of the failure of orthodox religions that as church attendances have dropped, and as the orthodox teachings have been found to have been formulated on false premises, so has the incidence of cancer increased.

The rules, doctrines, dogma and rituals of the Christian Church were designed to satisfy a peasant and illiterate congregation.

With universal education came not only the ability to read, but the gift of being able to reason. The myths, the fairy stories, the fictions that the Church perpetuated for so many years were no longer acceptable to a literate, reasoning people.

Unfortunately, they threw out the baby with the bathwater, and the basic philosophy of first century Christianity went out of the window, too.

Bereft of a workable philosophy, lacking any real spiritual leadership, men and women had no opportunity of discovering spiritual strength. Modern day stress had to be dealt with by bottling up emotions. Thus cancer found the environment in which to flourish.

It would take an historian and a better scholar than I to correlate the fall of religion with the rise of cancer, but it is there to see.

Spiritualism teaches we survive death, that we are responsible for what we do in this life, that there exists a brotherhood of man, and that love, tolerance and understanding are a common bond.

Teaching is not enough. What you are told is secondary knowledge. What you find out for yourselves is more important.

Spiritualism gives you the opportunity of finding out for yourselves, of communicating with those who have dedicated themselves to helping us, and of achieving personal spiritual awareness.

With this awareness comes the ability to control one's thoughts, actions, and philosophy, and to deal in a mature way with stress. Thus Spiritualism is a natural way to achieving a preventive philosophy that does not allow cancer to come into your life.

It is my sincere belief if a man or woman goes to a healer he can help them prevent having cancer. And that those who already have it can be healed; its spreading, its secondary infection, can be controlled.

Those who come to a healer after they have had the orthodox treatment of surgery, ray treatment and chemotherapy may not be healed since the cells have been killed off or because parts of the body have been surgically removed.

But to them the healer can offer a lessening of the symptoms, a removal of fear of death, a workable philosophy, and hope.

No healer should give advice. It is not his function.

If a person comes to me who has cancer and asks me if he should have all or some of the orthodox treatments I will not offer an opinion. I am not qualified to give one.

Nor can I claim to heal everybody who comes to me.

All I can do is to be available, to offer healing, and to give a sick person the opportunity of making up his own mind.

From my experience orthodox medical and surgical treatment of cancer and healing are not compatible. Some orthodox medical treatments do not inhibit healing. The methods surgeons and doctors use do.

It is up to the patient to make a decision. Maybe this is the crossroad that marks the most important moment in his life. Perhaps his decision as to whether to rely on spiritual healing or surgery is his moment of truth.